Mastering Your Scenes

Your Blueprint For Success

J. A. Cox

J.A.Cox
Wilmington, Delaware

Copyright © 2013 by J.A. Cox.

All rights reserved. No part of this publication may be reproduced, distributed or transmitted in any form or by any means, including photocopying, recording, or other electronic or mechanical methods, without the prior written permission of the publisher, except in the case of brief quotations embodied in critical reviews and certain other noncommercial uses permitted by copyright law. For permission requests, write to the publisher, addressed "Attention: Permissions Coordinator," at the address below.

J.A. Cox/ J.A. Cox
1207 Delaware Ave #2615
Wilmington, DE, 19806
jacoxbtih@gmail.com
www.jacoxbtih.com

Book Layout ©2013 BookDesignTemplates.com

Ordering Information:
Quantity sales. Special discounts are available on quantity purchases by corporations, associations, and others. For details, contact the "Special Sales Department" at the address above.

Mastering Your Scenes/ J.A. Cox. —1st ed.
ISBN 978-0-9895773-5-9

Contents

Introduction 7
    The Elements 7

    Archetypes Of Writers 8

What is a Scene? 11
    Sketching 12

LOCATION 17
    Primary Location 18

    Secondary Location 21

TIME 25
    Chronological Time 25

    Particular Time 28

CHARACTERS 31
    Primary Characters 32

    Indigenous Characters 34

PERSPECTIVE 39

God's Eye View	39
Character Point Of View	42
RESISTANCE	47
Internal Resistance	48
External Resistance	51
OBJECTIVE	55
Author's Objective	55
Scene Objective	58
BRINGING IT TOGETHER	61
Example Of A Scene Template	61
Example Of A Completed Template	66

I dedicate this book to K.M. Weiland for the inspiration I received from her vast knowledge that she shares helping writers become authors as well as my friends Graham and Tiffany for their support and allowing me to help with advice in Tiffany's book.

Don't allow your emotions to impede your chance to seize the opportunity before you.

—J. A.

Introduction

Have you ever felt passionate about something but didn't feel qualified to express your thoughts to others about it?

Have you ever read some information put forth by a professional but did not agree with all of their points but thought what do I know?

I have felt just like that and this book is the result of those feelings not standing in my way. Don't allow your emotions to impede your chance to seize the opportunity before you. I pray that within these pages you will find the inspiration to do just that.

These elements by no means need to be orchestrated in some specific pattern in order to be effective. Think of them as tools in a toolbox that you may find useful for a specific scene, while some may not fit, throughout the whole of your work I am sure they will benefit you greatly. However, I will let you be the judge of that.

The Elements

1. Sketching
2. Location
3. Time
4. Characters
5. Perspective
6. Resistance
7. Objective

Archetypes Of Writers

You will likely see yourself in one of these archetypes when it comes to putting these elements to use or maybe even more as you progress through your own writing as you utilize these techniques.

The Mad Scientist - for this person, the elements are chemicals that they will mix together for an amazing reaction that will tantalize and captivate their readers.

The Architect or Builder - for this person, the elements will become the blueprint or materials to erect their breath-taking structure that will shock and awe.

The Painter - for them, the elements are a palette of colors to blend together on the canvas of a blank page, displaying a masterpiece that touches the heart.

The Chef - for this one, each element is an ingredient to season the story to taste and be savored one bite at a time in the mouth of the reader.

The challenge is, do not limit yourself to some rigid perspective in utilizing these elements, but allow the archetype that desires release to be unleashed as you put them to work and be amazed by what you are left with. You may not resonate with the archetypes that I have named and that is okay, however you perceive these elements in your mind is what you want to go with, so that you end up with the masterpiece that you desire.

CHAPTER 1

What is a Scene?

Since this book is all about writing a scene, it would be a good idea to discuss what it is before we begin talking about how to build one. I am sure that you already have many ideas on how to answer the question above, but please humor me for now.

Let's look at a scene in this manner:
- As an episode.
- As a segment of an episode.

Some episodes are short, and some are long, it really all depends on how they are made. Also, an episode is the medium in which a portion of a series plays out. A scene can also be viewed in the same manner, as a medium in which a portion of your story plays out. On that notion, some may be short, and some may be long, but they still fulfill the same purpose. They provide the boundaries to contain all of the myriad of things that will take place at a certain point in the story.

Consider that within an episode that there are segments in which very particular things happen, such as a robbery at a bank, a high-speed chase along the highway or even a ship being boarded by pirates on the high seas. All of these segments placed into a written format would actually be the scene itself. I hope I am not confusing you but am just trying to convey the fact that a scene in a story fulfills the purpose of both episode and segment combined.

The purpose of this book is to look at the pieces that go into creating the segment so that you can create the most dynamic episode possible. Another very important factor about a scene, is its continuity. Whether one scene directly spills into the next or it is briefly interrupted as you transition to something else for a few scenes and pick back up where you left off, you still want things to be seamless. One of my goals is through the use of these elements to empower you with the ability to do so with ease. You can think of each element as a layer on which to build each scene in your story and as your story evolves your use of each will shift as some may not be needed and others will be essential. I will help you to realize how they all tie together to bring out the best in your scene creation.

Sketching

This may be the most overlooked aspect of the whole scene building process, but it should not be. While you may not always need to do so, it will help you to accomplish your greatest asset in writing, visualization. Never forget, artists by nature, especially writers, are very visual people. Of course, we must make an acceptation for the musician, but even their ability to hear those tunes in their mind is the same as any other artist being able to see what it is that they desire to create. I believe Michael Angelo stated something along the lines that he simply sculpted the David that he had already seen within the rock. This is my point, if you are trying to write on a blank sheet of paper with the idea that you are waiting for the words to just magically appear, you got it backwards. You first need to see the words that will be scribed or typed onto that blank sheet or document on the screen and then they will appear. In the movie, The Field of Dreams, the concept was the same, the voice had said, "If you make it, they will come." So, this is where sketching comes into play.

Rough Sketch

Definition - a quickly put together representation that just gives you an idea of what you desire to see.

Detailed Sketch

Definition - a very well put together representation of the place that you desire to see.

WHEN

With the rough sketch the whole idea is like brainstorming, you just want to get some idea of what that setting looks like, just enough for you to begin to really visualize it. It is helpful when you can't quite figure out how everything will fall into place but want to get the idea down and out of your head. This allows you to go back to it later and begin to add the skeletal structure and sinews and so on as you begin your detailed sketch. Keep in mind that you want to sketch as much as you feel it is necessary to prime that pump of visualization. Don't wait until you are ready to draft, you want to do this in your outlining and planning phase when you are considering the scene in particular. It is okay to suffice for a rough sketch in the outlining and planning phase but when it comes time to start drafting out that scene you will want to be working with your detailed sketch so you know exactly where things are going to be and where things can be such as pitfalls and such.

So, strive to use your rough sketch during outlining and the detailed for the drafting but it is really up to you, I am just giving you some ideas.

WHY

It helps your scene become more real to you. Consider this, the less real your scene is to you the harder it will be for you to convey that to your reader. If you have a bland scene then that means you need to go back to the drawing board and recreate that scene from the ground up until you can feel, breathe, see, hear etc. Does this make sense? The more the cellar in that haunted house gives you goosebumps, the more it will give your reader goosebumps. Also, this is where the detailed sketch is the most useful in fulfilling this purpose, a half thrown together idea of what things are supposed to look like is not going to cut it.

HOW

Let me clarify something, I am not just talking about you doing some doodling on a sheet of paper. Also, in order to prime the visual pump in your mind you may have to do a few things in order to do some doodling in the first place.

Things such as:
- Get out to a location that is similar and take pictures with a phone or camera or just bring some paper and begin to write down or draw out what you see.
- Surf the Internet and find pictures of similar locations.
- Find someone that you know that is knowledgeable about a similar location and pick their brains, taking lots of notes.
- Instead of drawing anything just use a picture from the Internet that is close in dimensions, naturally occurring things such as rocks, sticks, building etc. and use it as a base or template. Once you have accomplished this just alter the rest in your mind and remove what is not necessary and reshape it in your drafting to meet your own needs.
- I'm sure you can probably think of some other ways of priming that pump of visualization and no matter what way that is, as long as you realize that sometimes it is necessary to do so, that is what is important. If you do not, you will find yourself discouraged and frustrated that you cannot or at the worst end up writing out a scene that doesn't feel very real to you or your reader, but it has a lot going on. They may forgive you, but you will always know that you could have done much better. My aim is to help you to do much better from the start.

PRACTICAL APPLICATION

By first taking the time to implement one of the methods above this will prove invaluable for creating your locations. Location is the next element we will be dealing with and as you are considering a location you will want to be doing so in this phase. It is rather difficult to write about something that you can't really see that well. It is also boring to read about a place that doesn't feel unique or even real. It doesn't matter if the place is as abstract as they come if it does not feel real to you or your characters, it will not feel real to your readers. You must be convinced of how real the place is that you are writing about and I am not talking about going overboard in details, less is better. Immersion is the key and the key to immersion is the senses. That is why you may need to physically get out to a place that is similar to what you have in mind and breathe the air, experience perhaps the foul stench that protrudes from it or redolent aroma. Even hear the animal sounds firsthand and then you can distort them to your heart's desire in your writing, but now you will have had a firsthand experience. When you can't, just watch something and use your imagination.

The point is, that the foundation of visualizing the location, is in your sketching.

CHAPTER 2

LOCATION

Something unique to consider about a location is that every location comes along with its own indigenous obstacles.

Why do I mention this?

It is for the reason that once you really open your mind to this fact, that it naturally provides a variety of potential things to help or hinder your characters, especially as you seamlessly weave them into their path at those critical moments. It also helps your scene to naturally come to life and give you many potential ideas to put into place. For instance, if your primary location is a dense forest, various elements that will directly impact the characters would be animal life, tree branches, holes, spider webs and so on.

What if the primary location is a desert?

If so, you would have things such as: extreme heat for the day, cold at night, animals, and dehydration as a natural antagonist.

What about open space or the sky?

In these cases, I say use your imagination and choose the most realistic things that could be encountered. In open space besides having an asteroid belt in the scene there could be territories that are governed by certain races that may not take trespassing lightly and so on. Even in the sky, there are fowl, the wind currents, a decrease in oxygen, and even the velocity an aircraft is traveling, which could easily become a natural obstacle if it becomes damaged. Anyhow, I hope you get the point. Once again, it all comes down to a little bit of imagination with a splash of realism.

Another important aspect about location is during your brainstorming and outlining phase you want to get as specific as you can in identifying the locations in which your scenes will play out. The more precise, the easier it will be to plan out your scenes. This will make more sense later as we delve into the specifics. When it all comes down to it, just keep in mind that one way or another your locations should bear some significance to the overall plot or aide in propelling the story along.

Primary Location

Definition - the stage upon which your scene takes place.

The primary location will be the main place that a scene or scenes occur. For example, let's say that at a particular point in your Work in Progress that an entire chapter or chapters take place on a space cruise ship. That space cruise ship itself, while it is a location will become the primary location upon which all the scenes will unfold. However, the actual scenes will take place in departure stations, hallways, bedrooms, the bow, port, engine room and so on. All of these places we would classify as secondary locations and we will discuss those more in a few.

WHEN

How often you will be introducing a primary location into your story hinges on its necessity. It is easier to reuse a memorable location and have it create a more lasting impact on the reader than it is to bombard the reader with several locations throughout the entire story. But that hinges much on your style of writing as to how effective either case may be. Also, a single primary location could easily span the scope of several chapters. It really all depends on its significance to your story.

WHY

Every story takes place somewhere, therefore location is just a natural part of a scene, even if it is taking place in the sky.

HOW

The most important thing to take into consideration is what the importance of the location is. While every location does not have to leave a lingering impact on the consciousness of the reader, you at least want something worth remembering to take place. Either way, try to avoid having a location exist just for the sake of a scene taking place. Think of some logical reason for your locations, whether they exist for the purpose of slowing down your protagonist, helping them to face a fatal flaw so that they can achieve their goal or perhaps just giving them a breather before you crank the heat up so high they forgot they took that breath. In short let your chosen locations be on purpose, rather than by chance.

Example:

In the anime Sengoku Basra in the second season, one of the Main Characters Date, pronounced (Daw - tay) Masamune leads his troops to take down the main antagonist. However, at a specific place where in the past he witnessed his greatest failure as well as lost an eye, he was forced by another main character's soldiers to halt his advance. Instead of fighting this character's army he and his troops stopped for a break. The purpose of the opposing Lord was to force Date to think twice before he proceeded forward on his goal to face the main antagonist so that he would not repeat the failure he witnessed at that very place in days gone by.

I won't give away any more spoilers here, but the point is that this scene was important, not so much for the overall plot but more so to force this character to cool his jets so he did not run head long to his death. The significance is, that it had value to the character and added value to the story as it was also used to give us a little back story into that character.

I challenge you to give your locations value for being used other than to just be a place that your characters visited, or their feet have touched.

PRACTICAL APPLICATION

Below you will find a working copy of how you will be putting these elements to use in your scene outlining and planning. Keep in mind that what is below will go under the heading of Primary location.

CURRENT EVENTS

It would be here that you would list a general overview of things that are going on in the scene from the location as a whole. Even things that are not directly involved in the scene itself. Keep in mind that the primary location is the entire area including all secondary locations. By doing this you will be laying the foundation for everything that will be taking place, to a certain degree.

Example:

Let's say there was some kind of chemical outbreak that occurred in a prior scene. Even if we are not dealing with the same primary location the importance is the correlation these events have on our new scene. These are some of the things we would want to be considering:

1. How has it impacted the security?
2. Is the one responsible still at large?
3. Were there other conspirators working from the inside?
4. If so, what are they doing right now?
5. What is the person in charge doing?
6. What protocols have been set in place because of this?
7. How does any of the above help or hinder your characters?

Do you get the idea of what I am trying to convey here? Depending on the events prior, you want to consider how they impact the things that will happen in your next scene if they have a direct correlation. Perhaps there will be a dramatic shift from the events of one scene to another that does not directly relate to the one before it, but do those events play out later on in another scene? If so, then you will want to pick back up with the things that were going on and determine the impact on the new scene you are working on.

Does this make sense?

This is where the primary scene provides the most value to your scene writing, by helping you to nail down the big picture as it fits.

Secondary Location

Definition - The specific place in the primary location in which a scene unfolds.

WHEN

Whether you realize it or not this is the most used element in your fictional writing. All of the functioning parts of a scene play out here. Considering on the amount of activity that is taking place in a particular scene, it could encompass a single scene or many scenes. For instance, if you are writing a fantasy story and are dealing with a ball or gala scene in the grand hall, there may be things happening at tables, a stairwell or the center of the hall where there is dancing and so on. The scene may begin at a table, but the characters migrate to the dance floor, then to the stair well and I believe you get the point. This secondary location could encompass a single scene and even an entire chapter depending on the significance it has on your story or how large it is. Therefore, it may not be necessary to have too many secondary locations as you can also recycle them and alter their set up here and there if they are revisited over a long stretch of time or short stretch. R.A. Salvatore uses this method in a particular town in his books that is rife with pirate lords. At one point in the stories the town is thriving and years down the road it is overrun with different factions vying for power. Natural disasters are also a good way to recycle secondary locations and drastically alter their appearance to the point it is like it is a whole new place.

WHY

The primary location is just the stage or outer shell but the skeleton, sinews and so on represents the secondary location. You may have not been looking at your locations in this manner but it is my hope that you will from now on and that it will transform the way you look at them and help to unlock greater levels of creativity within you.

HOW

First of all, just as you want more of a reason for your primary location to exist than to just be some random place the characters visit, you want the same to be for your secondary location. Now, let's do a little dissecting. Let's say that our primary location is a thieves den. Therefore, all of the rooms, hidden as well as visible, hallways, closets and so on consist of our secondary locations. Now, consider what rooms stand out the most.

Which rooms or places within have the most significance to our characters and plot?

Where do the darkest and most secretive of meetings take place there?

What are the places that only the most loyal can lay eyes?

Are you starting to follow me?

This is the line of thought you want to generate as you plan out your scene or even when working on your world building and back story as you set up your outline.

PRACTICAL APPLICATION

Under the heading of secondary location, you will want to list out the details of this place. This is where the description comes into place. Also, this is where the sketching especially the detailed sketch is going to be a great asset to you.

Ask questions such as:
1. What does it smell like?
2. What is the weather like?
3. What type of sounds would you hear?
4. What type of lighting is there?
5. What color is the sky?
6. What type of terrain is there?
7. What type of people are there?
8. What type of animals are there?
9. What type of layout does it have?

Hopefully, you understand that the main functionality of the secondary location is the details. It is here that you get into the nitty gritty of that scene as far as placement of things and people are concerned. Talking about placement, this is also where our next element is going to be of great value, when you are working on this portion. That element is time, but we will discuss those details in the next chapter. Either way, you should notice that these elements have an overlapping ability to them and tend to work in concert with one another in helping you to achieve your masterpiece. While this will not be the case every time, I think you will be surprised how often that it is so.

CHAPTER 3

TIME

So, what is so important about time?

In a word, pacing. Time can really accentuate the pacing of your scene. It becomes the driving force that carries the character along in certain scenes. A very good example of this is in the beginning of the book Oxygen written by John B. Olson and Randy Ingermanson. At the start of the book one of the main characters are forced to find interesting ways to get oxygen into their lungs due to a precarious situation they find themselves in. The insignificant amounts of oxygen they are provided with as they move from one thing to the next is the driving force of the first few scenes of this book. Therefore, the time here is signified in the amount of oxygen they have until they die from a lack there of, considering that the air is contaminated to the point that it doesn't have a sufficient amount to offer them.

During this section I will provide you with two types of time for use in your scenes.

Chronological Time

Definition - the measurement of hours, minutes, and such.

I know it is not very profound but breaking it up and looking at it in such a way will be invaluable to you for your scene planning.

WHEN

The use of this element varies depending on what you have planned. In the movies this would be useful for burglars planning their great heist of the century. The information on what hour that armored car is going to be headed down a particular road and what the amount of traffic is likely to be at that hour and so on would be taken into consideration, to hijack it. The same goes for the infiltration of a heavily guarded facility. Knowing where those guards will be at a given moment or the hour their shifts change and the hours that their mark would be occupying that facility are all need to know details. Therefore, this is where looking at your scene in this way as you are putting that outline together comes in handy. With that in mind you are able to make the heist more realistic and of course you are not going to make it a cake walk for your thieves, someone will forget about the one minor detail that happens to derail the whole plan, just as it seems to be a cake walk.

Are you starting to see the potential this type of thinking will bring to your scenes?

I hope so.

WHY

We pretty much covered the reason above. Just like with the example in the Oxygen book it does not necessarily have to be minutes that are ticking down on a clock but could be the duration that a person has before they run out of oxygen. The point is you need to really be as imaginative with this element as possible to get the best use out of it.

HOW

Example: (From my Sci-Fi book, Fulfilling a Vow: Searching for Answers.)

"Die Manit-" Utentherin gargled. Orange-brown blood exuded from a smoldering hole in his throat. <u>The characters, still in dual digits, counted down rapidly.</u>

Turning to escape Manitra slammed down into the floor. Utentherin had managed to grab hold of her legs with one massive hand, his final act of defiance as the last remnants of his life ebbed into eternity. <u>The characters on the display raced on into single digits, continuing their mocking pace.</u>

While there is no specific mention of time, the shifting of those characters from dual digits down to single digits and moving at a mocking pace creates the ideal that Manitra does not have very much time until her impending doom. Although I don't describe the characters, you understand clearly that they represent seconds counting down which encompasses the essence of what chronological time is. Whatever you call it for your own particular writing needs is fine by me.

PRACTICAL APPLICATION

Besides being helpful with pacing time is also essential for our character placement, especially for the indigenous characters, we will cover them in the next chapter. Time is not the only element that helps with character placement, but it gives you an idea where they will be during a certain period. This is going to have a lot to do with what you have going on in your scene. Either way it is good to be considering this from the aspect of the primary location. Even if a certain group of characters may not be in the scene, just knowing that they will be in a specific area by your primary or secondary character could be useful information for decisions that character will make. Your primary character realizing that the antagonist will be returning to their office at a particular time that they just so happen to be snooping around in could make them a little sloppy in their search, causing them to leave behind evidence that will haunt them later.

Keep in mind that these are the types of questions you will be trying to address underneath your Chronological time heading; these are just enough to prime your pump:
1. What time of day is it?
2. Are there any significant activities taking place?
3. Are there any events going on that will impede the goals of the primary or secondary characters?

4. How many people will be in certain areas during a specific time?
5. Who will those people be?
6. How great will their impact be to what goal that the primary or secondary character needs to accomplish?

Particular Time

Definition - time based on specific events or periods such as festivals, holidays, inaugurations, ceremonies, and the like.

WHEN

The most important thing here is to think about all of those important events that will take place in your story as a whole or scene and begin to brainstorm. Things such as festivities, characters that are likely to be present, what factions those characters are part of and what moves they are likely to make during an event of that nature are examples of this to be considered. Looking at your scene from this angle will help you to brainstorm better and consider things you might not have otherwise.

WHY

It is to help you get a better perspective of the possibilities or potential you have to work with in a given scene. By focusing in on the scene from this perspective it allows you to consider what is going on from an angle you may not otherwise see it from. It is easy to get tunnel vision when you are working on your scenes and end up with something that is okay but could have been much more immersing if you would had stepped back a little further and looked at it again.

HOW

A good example of this playing out in a scene is in the first Kung Fu Panda movie during the Dragon warrior selection festival.

Before Pho hastily took off to go get a glimpse of the festivities his father sneakily donned an apron around his waist and urged him to take the noodle cart.

While it may be a simple illustration keep this in mind. Pho's father ran a restaurant and the big event meant that there would be a large crowd of hungry customers which would equal a big profit for him to maximize. Of course, on the other hand this meant that the next dragon warrior would also be selected. So, the use of this element presents two separate opportunities. If you happened to have watched the movie you already know which opportunity played out over the other. The point of this is giving yourself the ability to have a few opportunities to unfold within your scene which at first one may seem to be a given to your reader but then you turn around and pull the floor from under them.

PRACTICAL APPLICATION

This element of time does not really do much to aide in the pacing of a scene as it does the placement of characters in a scene. So, for the particular time section of your outlining you will solely be focused on things such as:

1. What are the special events that are going on at the location? (Don't limit your mind to just holidays, think board meetings, briefings, meetings in general and so on.)
2. Who will be in attendance at these special events?
3. What impact will these events have on the location or in the scene?
4. How will these events impede or aide your primary or secondary characters?

CHAPTER 4

CHARACTERS

While it is well understood what characters are, I wish to focus on the actual use of characters and their importance to a scene in general. Also, when it comes to choosing characters for the sake of adding more depth to your scene you will want to adopt the habit of not placing several compatible characters together in one scene. Yes, they may have to work together to achieve a singular objective but make sure that their personalities are very diverse. This is what makes the Guardians of the Galaxy such a good example to use for this. They are a complete mash up of characters that give you the feel that they were just thrown together. That naturally makes for plenty of entertainment as there is always going to be some type of resistance taking place which could be used to propel the scene along. However, I am not saying that this should always be your goal because you can have likeminded characters that have completely opposing viewpoints on something but still the opposition in their thinking is the element that will help to develop things on a deeper level. Your goal should always be to utilize those differences in the characters to deepen the experience the reader feels for that scene you are working on.

I'm going to break down character usage into two categories although in an essence I will be speaking of three different categories, but you will understand shortly.

Primary Characters

Definition- The characters you will be placing the most emphasis on.

Keep this in mind, that when I use the term primary it is inclusive to both secondary and primary characters. I say this because at times as your scenes evolve one of your intended secondary characters may take on the primary role just for that scene or it could be a chapter. We will discuss this a little more shortly.

WHEN

Alright, the placement of characters has much to do with another element aside from secondary location and time, Character Point of View. We will get more in depth about it in the upcoming chapter. The placement I speak of has to do with the beginning, middle or end of a scene. In short it is a matter of a character's perspective that the scene will be viewed from by the reader. So, determining which character's perspective the scene needs to initially be viewed from should be your litmus test of deciding if you will go with the primary, secondary or even the indigenous character. Also, you want to consider if it would be more beneficial to use one characters point of view or more throughout the scene. Less is better but if it would fit to use more than one than by all means do so. Yes, it could get a little tricky so if things just get too difficult stick with one character.

WHY

These are the characters that your readers are going to be identifying with the most.

How

Example: (From my Sci-Fi book, Fulfilling a Vow: Searching for Answers.)

Danatha Manitra, Danatha!" shouts her tapha. He shoved his dotha into a hidden compartment in a nearby wall. The somber gaze of his, jade-green eyes fell heavy upon her pudgy, caramel-brown face. They looked upon her as the scrupulous eyes of a sculptor on a block of stone awaiting nimble hands to bring forth the masterpiece that lay within. Her little eyes opened wide like shimmering pools touched by the moon's pale light; pools that reflected the stoical look imprinted on his face. She shivered. The most horrid thought emerged.

Tapha.

Her mouth parted but the words were lost to her. Manitra's small, slender fingers trembled as they reached out to him. It crushed her to see the crystalline beads welling up in his eyes. How she wished to wipe them away, but he had already begun closing the door. Their eyes were locked until the soft click of the latch echoed, enveloping her in darkness. It was ironic that the secret compartment she had so often used to hide away would protect her. The soft luminance of her lavender-purple eyes lit the surrounding darkness like the gentle light of a burning candle.

In the scene above it should be clear that the character point of view is from the eyes of the girl Manitra. Can you tell from this passage that she has a deep reverence and love for her father? While it is also very clear that this man really cares for his daughter it is vital to the plot that she is the character in which things are viewed from. This is the defining moment that will spur many things into motion in the future for her and make for one very high paced adventure. While the point of view of the father could have easily been used it would not have the same impact on the reader as the story progressed. So, it was vital to establish her feelings toward him as this is the last time, he will be interacting with her in this way. Sorry for the semi-spoiler but I assume that you would pick that up anyhow. Also, the rest of this scene is completely through her senses in order for the reader to fully grasp what was the forge that had shaped this girl into what she becomes later on.

PRACTICAL APPLICATION

These are the types of questions you may want to ask yourself under the primary character heading in your scene outline:

1. Which character will help create the greatest immersion experience at the start of the scene?

2. Which character will help create the greatest immersion experience at the middle of the scene?
3. Which character will help create the greatest immersion experience at the end of the scene?
4. Would the use of a single character achieve the greatest immersion experience for this scene?

Indigenous Characters

Definition - The characters that act as a backdrop, they are a natural occurring factor of a particular setting.

WHEN

Just think of putting on a play on a stage in a forest scene with no tree props, grass props, animal props and so on. It would really make for a very bland performance. First of all, let's talk about where these characters originate from. In order to do this, we will need to reach back to the chapter about location.

Location will be your litmus test to determine:
1. How many there will be.
2. What type of characters they should be?
3. What is the role they will play?

So, location, both primary and secondary will be a great asset in the placement of these characters as well as the element of time. This will be discussed further under the how.

WHY

These characters provide more depth to a scene when their use is necessary. They also could provide a great means of entertainment as they shine in the spotlight for that short period of time and can also help to place greater emphasis on how bad that villain is or heroic the hero or heroine is. While the reasons can vary when they are included, they really add a great deal of value. Consider this, if you go to a jungle, you naturally expect to see a certain variety of animals. So, when you are writing about a particular location, your readers should expect to see, hear, and feel those elements that are naturally occurring there as it fits.

HOW

Also, keep in mind that you can discuss indigenous characters as a group or as an individual, it really depends on what is most useful for a scene in particular. You may find yourself referring to an entire group as if it were to be a character itself, think of the mob mindset. Most people in a mob behave the same because they are mimicking the actions of a single individual. Therefore, the mob now becomes a single entity to describe although it is made up of numerous people whom it is not important to mention on an individual level. You can use this for any groups of people and just make a general reference as to what they are doing. With that said, let's discuss the importance of location in helping us with indigenous character placement. For example, let's say that our primary location is a bank located in the downtown district of a certain city. We would want to think about the type of people we would naturally expect to find there.

So, let's do a little brainstorming:
- We will have tellers.
- We will have loan officers.
- We will have customers.
- We may have security personnel.
- We may have contractors of various types conducting business for the bank like repairs and so on.
- We may have your random shady person or even mentally displaced individual who happens to come trotting in.

The above represents more of a general overview of who to expect from a primary location perspective. Now when you begin to look at things from the perspective of a secondary location you are looking at where these characters will be.

Think of it this way:
- Tellers are most likely to be found behind a counter.

- Loan officers are most likely to be found at a desk in a designated area.
- Customers waiting on a loan officer will be in a designated seating area.
- Customers waiting on the tellers will be in a line in front of the tellers.
- Contractors will be wherever they need to be to conduct their business.

Is it becoming clear how location is your cheat sheet to help with the natural placement of your indigenous characters? It really is just a little matter of thought of what makes the most sense. Even if we were talking about a neighborhood, while things would not be so cut and dry the placement is pretty straightforward. Even though you know some kids will be in the street, there will be others riding bikes, skateboards, roller blades at random at any given point. You will have vehicles in driveways, and some being washed by their owners and so on. Still you will have a basic idea of placement. This does not mean you cannot for the purpose of your scene objective alter the placement as you see fit, but it helps to have an idea of how it should generally look in order to do so.

Now with all that said, along with location, time is a very important piece in determining the exact placement of an indigenous character in a location. Just think about it, security will always have shift changes, employees will break for lunch even if it is at a desk while they have a so-called working lunch. I think you get the idea here. Even if there is a special event like Memorial Day you know that certain places like department stores and what not are going to be flooded with customers and especially parks will be brimming with activity. Let's not forget on certain significant days there may be parades or even fairs. This is where time comes in as well as the type of indigenous characters that will happen to be a part of that scene just because of this.

PRACTICAL APPLICATION

So, under the heading of indigenous characters you will want to ask questions along these lines:

1. How many are necessary?
2. At what time would certain characters be expected to be at certain places?
3. What would they be doing at these locations?
4. How would their activities help or hinder the objective of the primary or secondary characters?

CHAPTER 5

PERSPECTIVE

Just think of perspective as being synonymous with point of view, the angle in which you see something from. I am persuaded that in fiction, you are only dealing with two distinct point of views. Before I get into what they are let's discuss the significance of point of view in your scene.

That significance can be explained with one word, realism. It is with this element that you help your reader to care about your characters and story. Perspective is the entry point that draws the readers mind from reality into your fantasy realm and causes them to build an empathic link with your characters. At least that is what your aim should be with the use of it. It is also a crucial element that helps you to mold the mind of your reader into the image that you desire and that will be the case if you get it right. My goal is to help you achieve exactly that.

God's Eye View

Definition - A zoomed out view of the things taking place in the scene.

WHEN

Keep in mind that this will encompass things the character may not be actively aware of. Therefore, this is most useful at the start of a scene when you want to: describe the interior or exterior of a location, incorporate lighting, smells, and so on. It also does well for giving a general feel for a situation unfolding in a scene such as a large-scale battle. Of course, you would naturally shift to the individual skirmishes taking place in which the second point of view comes into play in order to capture the feel of the battle. However, during that battle you may have one character fighting their way through the hordes to aide another in which you can zoom out and encompass all of the gore around them as they wade deeper into the chaos to get to them. This would give the reader or viewer a broader scope as to the scale of devastation that has unfolded.

Example:

While this doesn't exactly follow suite with what I am speaking of it still conveys the same idea. Near the end of the movie Willow there is a large scale battle in which the camera zooms out at one point to focus on the body of a close ally of Mad Martigen that rolls down a slope after being defeated by the enemy general. Then the camera shifts to Mad Martigen taking notice of the rolling body. He quickly runs to their aide and there is a brief focus on their dialog before the ally takes his final breath. After this the camera zooms out to show the enemy general slaying other ally soldiers as he moves in the opposite direction, then Mad Martigen pursues him with vengeance.

The significance of this, is that this Point of View may or may not involve things within the immediate senses of the character. Earlier, before the close ally was slain the camera focuses on his brief fight with the enemy general which takes place out of the line of sight of Mad Martigen.

WHY

The necessity of its use varies greatly but a very simple reason to use this is for foreshadowing. It works well for that subtle tip off to the reader that something wicked this way comes whether they really pick up on it or not.

Example:

A few minutes into Kung Fu Panda 2 we have a God's Eye View of the wolves pillaging villagers and the camera briefly stops and zooms in a little on an insignia worn on the shoulder plate of a wolf's armor. Next the camera shifts to Pho standing on a mountain before he engages the wolves. Not long after he attacks that same wolf he freezes as he sees that insignia and has a flash back into his past about something very important that happened to him.

The whole point of mentioning that example is that it is foreshadowing of a significant event that hits very dear to him and has much to do with the main antagonist. Of course, as the movie goes on all the missing gaps are filled and you have the full picture by the end of the movie of its meaning. But they took a moment to tip off the audience in a subtle way and you would not think much of it until his reaction. Either way it is exactly the type of thing you can use with the God's Eye View to tip off your reader to something of that level, that the character at the time is not privy to.

HOW

Think of this as more of a placement issue rather than a specific order of events. That placement really depends on which is going to help your reader identify the most with the story or character or give the most realism to your prose. The easiest way to conclude what is best is to ask yourself if it adds or takes away from the scene. If you feel that it adds than keep it but if not get rid of it. If you are just unsure than find someone you respect and ask them the same question. There may be times when it is best to use this Point of View immediately following Character Point of view for transition purposes.

Example: (Excerpt from my Sci - Fi book Fulling A Vow: Searching for Answers)

Manitra leaped from the roof. A soft hum permeated the air as her hover boots came to life swiftly propelling her above the expressway below. Brakes screeched and horns honked as the traffic jerked its way along the road during rush hour. A few angry threats from exasperated and impatient occupants were hurled followed by waving hands with obscene gestures. Yet, no eyes seemed to notice the crimson donned beauty vanish from view. Red, nylon like fabric and caramel-brown skin alike rippled into a shimmering shroud of optical camouflage as clear as the air itself.

First of all, the focus starts off on the action Manitra is taking. We have her leaping from the top of a building juxtaposed to a busy expressway in which she will cross via hover boots. Now it is from here that we take a God's eye view of the actions taking place on the expressway. These are things that she is not privy to and surely could care less about since her objective lies on the other side of the expressway. Through the use of this element instead of just telling about the expressway, it is brought to life by briefly focusing on it until we return to the action of the character. The action is that Manitra disappears from sight and then we cut straight to the next scene. So, you now have an additional use for this element. That is to breathe life into a portion of a scene that could easily be considered insignificant but when done right it creates a greater feel of realism. Of course, that all depends on your writing style as it would have been fine to just have her jump from the building and fade out and cut right to the next scene but that is not my style. Instead of just cutting off when they leap from the building, by using the God's Eye View, we get a glimpse of the current activities taking place as she vanishes into thin air several feet above them.

PRACTICAL APPLICATION

These are the types of questions you will want to consider asking under the God's Eye view heading of your scene outline:
1. At which point of the scene will this be the most useful?
2. What is it you are trying to convey to the reader by doing so?

Character Point Of View

Definition - A first person perspective of the scene events.

WHEN

Even if you write from the third person perspective like I do, it is still possible to create the first person feel. I also believe that when you do so it allows for the reader to easily identify with the plight of your characters. So, keep in mind that this is not indigenous to one character but all of your characters. This is useful in any situation that you are not applying the God's eye View. I am persuaded that this is the most crucial element that will allow your readers to create the deepest bond with your characters. Also, when done right the reader will naturally experience all things through the character's senses because you will not be giving them much of a choice to do otherwise. The majority of your story would do well to be written from this perspective to create the most immersing environment.

Also, as I mentioned in the previous chapter it helps us to determine whether we will be using a primary or secondary character as that viewpoint character.

WHY

It is important to use this perspective to do one thing, help the reader to identify with your characters. Think of it this way, the less your readers identify or can identify with your characters the less they are going to care about your story. I would surmise that this is not why you began writing your Work in Progress. Aside from that, your readers can have the experience of being utterly terrified by the antagonist as they see his cruelty first hand through the eyes of perhaps a captain witnessing his team getting slaughtered until he is the last man standing and you abruptly end the scene leaving them in suspense just as he brings the captain into submission. It also works very well in the start of your story when you want your reader to experience the tragic moment that sets it all into motion through the body of your Main Character as they witness with abject horror the brutal destruction of their loved ones before their very ears or eyes. Is it beginning to come together better for you?

HOW

It is here that you either will make or break that identification or imprint on the consciousness of your reader. In order to do this right, you must focus on the use of emotional stimulation. Basically, don't come right off the bat with telling the reader your characters are sad, mad, or terrified. Do so after you have shown them the subtle signs through gestures or internal responses and build it up to a crescendo. So, really take some time to think and even observe some of those telltale signs that precede these various emotions and mix them in with thoughts as well as speech.

Example: (Excerpt from my Sci - Fi book Fulling A Vow: Searching for Answers)

Ranthorus shot to his feet and vanished. <u>Brynz's mouth fell open</u> at the sound of the blood curdling shriek, his eyes drawn to the horrific scene before him. He saw the languid form of one of his men impaled by Ranthorus' hand, his hulking figure lifted with ease by that scaled, gaunt limb. There he hanged as Ranthorus fully extended his arm holding the body above his head, now in plain view since his bio signs were no longer high enough to keep his stealth operational. Ranthorus' <u>pupil less eyes also looked upon Brynz enjoying that wide eyed gaze of disbelief</u>, as he whipped his arm down and bounced the corpse against the floor before he vanished.

At the start we view Ranthorus through Brynz's eyes. Although there is not much detail about his internal thoughts or physiological changes aside from his mouth hanging open, the description of the horror that is Ranthorus conveys the feeling he is experiencing. Hence one way of displaying the emotions and feeling of the characters is through the allusion to what they witness. I believe it is very clear that he is in some state of shock, compounded by his facial expression viewed through the eyes of Ranthorus at the end. That feeling only builds and his emotions shift from one end of the spectrum to the other and back before the scene is finished. The point here is that Ranthorus comes off as a force not to be taken lightly to the reader as well as the character. Aside from that, since Brynz is the commander of this group it does more for the reader to witness the slaughter of his team through his eyes. It would not be the same seeing such through his subordinates unless he was the only one that was going to be killed.

PRACTICAL APPLICATION

Under the heading of character point of view, you will basically ask the same questions you did under the primary character portion. Realize this, that when you are dealing with the primary character element you are also dealing with Character Point of view. It would be very helpful to you to think of the two as being synonymous. I am saying that you will not need a separate heading unless you really want one and can add this information into the portion under primary character.

CHAPTER 6

RESISTANCE

I am persuaded that too often this is synonymously used with physical conflict. I believe that the catalyst to writing your story from start to finish is the Resistance factor. How well you work with it will make it easier or more difficult to get things moving along. However, what matters the most about resistance is the motivating factor or factors behind it. For the Character to deal with these factors they must acknowledge that they exist. That does not mean that they will not be dealing with the repercussions of them even if they are in denial. A lot of times we don't realize our own struggles with something that we have been suppressing as we project it onto something or someone else. So, it is reasonable that your characters are going to do the exact same things. That is our job as the author to place them in situations where they have the opportunity to look into themselves. By doing so, we help them to realize who they are really fighting against. Upon that revelation we help them to understand that they must make reparations for the ones that they have been taking things out on if they have not killed them. That in itself makes for an interesting story.

Another thing to note, is that all the preceding elements will naturally generate and exacerbate these two types of resistance that we will be discussing below.

Internal Resistance

Definition - the psychological phantoms from past losses, failures, traumas and so on that rise up in the present to hinder the actions of your characters.

WHEN

You want to use this near the beginning of your story and throughout its entirety. While it may or may not be clear to the reader what they or it is, it can be shown through the way the character responds to situations they find themselves in. It is this resistance that pushes them from their comfort zone to embark on their long journey. It could be their feeling of being born for a greater purpose but being taught by their parents that it is their lot in life to accept their inferior status due to some philosophy passed on by their own parents. Maybe it is a burning desire for revenge because they refuse to accept their inability to have prevented the death of a loved one. The whole idea that if they had been stronger or had been present, that things would have been different and to amend this, they must seek the death of those responsible. Or maybe a great legend failed, and many died but a time arises in the future where they are the only one who is strong enough to turn the tide, however; that failure shackles them to the past and they refuse to assist the downtrodden. Of course, in such a scenario a secondary character would play the role of the persistent individual to help the legend realize that they need to get over themselves before their lack of action creates a greater catastrophe than their bad decision in the past did. Wouldn't it be something for the antagonist in such a plot to be a survivor of that horrible choice, one which is not revealed to the legend until the most crucial moment. Don't forget about me if I gave you the next great idea for your next best seller. Character point of view will be the element that will aide you the most in the usage of this. It will be due to its nature of taking you into the very skin of the character you are dealing with, which is exactly what the internal resistance has much to do with. So, through its use you want to take the opportunity to really poke around inside the characters head and irritate those suppressed emotions or traumas or past hurts and failures. Be as cruel as necessary if you want a great outcome.

WHY

The way your character deals with this type of resistance allows their personality to be seen and further developed. It also clearly shows the flaws in their nature which can be pointed out by other characters they encounter. The response to this will give some foreshadowing to the reader of how this character will deal with certain situations or how they will likely respond. This is where you must create situations for that character in which their natural way of responding would not work and force them to choose another means, although they would prefer to do what they naturally would do.

HOW

Example: (An excerpt from my sci-fi book Fulfilling a Vow - Searching for Answers)

The entire surface beneath that silver Venetian mask lit up like the underbelly of a vehicle fixed with fluorescent, neon bulbs. It was piercing lavender rays that were diffused by the noon day sun and further shielded by Manitra's downward turned face. Her stomach churned like an erupting volcano setting her chest aflame. Her bottom lip quivered beneath teeth sunken in so deep they almost drew blood. She agreed with those whispered comments that she did not belong in such a venue, decked out in such finery amongst affluent personalities that ranged from wealthy business professionals, foreign dignitaries as well as Operations Officers of the Earth Defense Force ranked OP 3 - 4 up to the Command Marshall himself. Never had she been so visible, so out in the open, so vulnerable. Embraced in the mantle of subterfuge and darkness, that was her forte but this, this was *bwangal,* an Etherenian word used to describe something wasteful, in excess or just not necessary. Her chest rose as the oxygen from that next inspiration sunk deep into her lungs, loosening tensed muscles, and allowing clenched fists full of emerald-green chiffon to unfurl. She remembered her reason for attending, her purpose for agreeing to remain with Suzuko at the hotel until they were picked up by the ebony - black limo and met up later with Fumiko and Makoto aboard the vessel. Yes, she remembered and straightened her slouch and held her head high just as Fumiko had instructed her. All that mattered was that she would get answers, maybe enough to assemble those scattered puzzle pieces into something more complete. So, she would endure the ridicule and disdain, for now.

I know it is quite a bit of reading, but it perfectly conveys what I mentioned about putting a character in a particular situation in which their normal behavior towards an external resistance aggravates the internal resistance, but they are forced to respond differently. What I did not put in there is that prior to what is above, that she had just recovered herself from a very embarrassing encounter with the hot pavement while being all decked out for this Gala event. Her flashing eyes are a natural indication of her level of irritation, the angrier she becomes the greater the intensity. It is a part of her alien physiology and very specific to her race. So, with that you have the first sign of her struggle with that internal resistance. You realize quickly that she has been ridiculed by other guests who are more accustomed to this type of affair. This is made even more clear in the description that she works alone from the shadows. Her lack of interpersonal skills makes her current situation very difficult to manage and then there is the fact that she sticks out like a sore thumb and has become a very public spectacle. She is used to just destroying the obstacles in her way with extreme prejudice and has absolutely all the power to do so but that would become an even greater obstacle in this environment and ruin her reason for being there in the first place. So, she decides to suppress those urges to annihilate her aggressors, considering that the only wound she has received is to her pride. If you think that I let up on her after that you have another thing coming, I push every button until she finally snaps but you will have to get yourself a copy of the book if you wish to find out what happened.

PRACTICAL APPLICATION

Remember that I mentioned earlier about other elements helping to aide in assisting the impact of resistance. This is where you will put them into place. You will want to ask the appropriate questions that will allow you to glean from them, such as:
1. What things in the environment could be factors that deepen the impact of the internal resistance?
2. How would they be used to do so?
3. How does the chronological time play a role in its effect on the internal resistance?
4. How does the particular time play a role in its effect on the internal resistance, such as the actual event or events taking place?
5. How many indigenous characters will be used to effect the internal resistance?
6. How will they be used to do so?
7. How can you use the character perspective to deepen the impact of the internal resistance?

External Resistance

Definition - the outward obstacles that stand between your characters and their goal or goals.

WHEN

Just like the other element this will be used around the start of your story and in about every scene thereafter. One thing to keep in mind, is that this is naturally developed as your character struggles to cope with the internal resistance they are dealing with. It is the opposite but opposing reaction from the decisions they made at the very start and then like a snowball it will only build and at times it may seem to have gone away only for them to be blindsided by an avalanche. So, from the very first scene you need to keep in mind how other characters and organizations are likely to respond to your characters decisions, this is where it is going to manifest. Also, your location both primary and secondary are going to play the greatest role in determining what those outward obstacles are because they should be naturally occurring within the environment. Don't get me wrong, this does not mean that you can't have a meteor come crashing down during that inaugural speech you have planned, but just make sure it works into the plot as well as the objective of that scene, unless it is the authors objective to foreshadow things yet to come. Anyhow, I think you get my point.

WHY

Without it you are not going to have much of a story. And if you don't have enough of it the interest in your story is going to die very quickly. However, you need not go overboard with it either. Remember it is the opposite but equal reaction to something your character has already set in motion. Maybe they did not even set it into motion but perhaps it was a loved one who is now deceased and just because they are affiliated with them, somebody is out to exact a payment out of their hide to get their money. So now you have another good reason for its use and a way to put it to work for you. The bottom line is that you do not want to treat it as something that just happens. You need to have a good reason for it so that interest will be kept. That is simple to accomplish when it involves something done by your character or someone affiliated with them. Think of it like guilt by association or maybe they wore the wrong colors in the wrong place at the wrong time. Are you starting to understand how easy this can be with some thought? Then there is always the occasional accident that occurs with the wrong person who is happening to have a bad hair day at that moment and you are now the object of their venting.

HOW

Example: (Excerpt from my sci - fi book Fulfilling a Vow: Looking for Answers)

Darryl Polanski, the board Committee Chair slapped the dossier hard against the table, ejecting a few sheets that fluttered in the air as the rest cascaded to the floor.

"What kind of rubbish is this?" OP Marshall Johnson bristled and braced for what followed with a tight grin. "Are we to believe that this saboteur traversed six miles in three minutes as well as took down 3 state of the art space fighter crafts flown by ace pilots and a rover full of six more pilots armed with heavy blasters, bare handed and alone?" <u>He shook his head and tossed up his hands.</u>

"Sir, that is firsthand information from the pilots themselves," he defended.

"I'm sorry but I don't buy it, not only did she deflect laser cannon blasts but missiles also," <u>-He wagged his head-</u> "my fellow board members, we have a press conference within the hour and if we don't come up with something better than this circus act of a report our shares are going to plummet and Goulen Industries and all of the work we've been conducting on the moon over the last decade or so is going to go up in smoke."

While the example above is not a physical fight scene the opposition displayed by Mr. Polanski is clear in his gestures that mirror his dialog. The board meeting in this particular scene that this was taken from is a direct result of the actions of the main character of this story. This ties into what I spoke of about the external resistance being the opposite but equal reaction. Although in this case it is not happening directly to the character the decisions made here will impact the character later on in this story. Also, the resistance of Polanski to accept the information passed on to him only creates more resistance from the one reporting later on in this scene and things only continue to heat up as the scene plays out in its entirety.

CONSIDER THIS

A very important thing about resistance both internal and external is that it is very easy to compound it. That should be your goal just as any good investor seeks out that compounded interest. So, once you have it going you want to keep it going, building it up until a final explosive moment that could either die down or you end it with everything all worked up as high as possible.

This is the beauty of propelling your story along. The better you learn to do this the faster or slower the pace of things will get. There needs to be a natural rise and flow to the fight, be it verbal or physical, or mental or a mix of all three. Really at least two are always in tandem no matter what the situation. Try to be upset without thinking of something bitter to say, even if you don't let it out you still experience the bitterness. The point is as one character throws a verbal jab something needs to happen from one or more characters to throw wood on that fire.

Also, an easy way to immediately bring a halt to building resistance is with an interruption of some sort. It could be some character bursting in right as things are literally about to go off the charts stating there is an emergency, or someone suddenly just passes out followed by others in rapid succession due to some unseen chemical emitted into the air and so on. Interruption is the key to bring any situation that is out of hand under control.

PRACTICAL APPLICATION

For external resistance you want to focus on what role the location will provide in determining the level of resistance. So, your questions will look more like this:

1. How many things in this location will be useful in hindering/aiding the primary character?
2. In what way will they be used to do so?
3. How many indigenous characters will be useful in hindering/helping the primary character?
4. What role do they play in that scene or location in general?
5. In what way will they be used to do so?
6. How many secondary characters will be useful in hindering/helping the primary character?
7. What role do they play in that scene or location in general?
8. In what way will they be used to do so?

CHAPTER 7

OBJECTIVE

Just like with the other elements there are two types of Objectives that can be used in a scene, either in tandem or stand alone. While you may have not looked at it in such a way, I am persuaded that when you do it gives you a more substantial reason for justifying some of those things that at a glance may be considered fluff. Or something in particular that you feel is important to have added but it doesn't really have anything to do with the plot and because of this you may feel torn between keeping it or discarding it. This is where the importance of the first type of objective comes into play.

Author's Objective

Definition - the authors goal for the scene.

WHEN

It is most beneficial to be used in a scene to place emphasis on something in particular. It could be something along the lines of the vast difference in abilities between the protagonist and the antagonist. Let's just say that it has already been made clear to the reader how powerful your protagonist is and that their goal is to get revenge on the antagonist for the death of a loved one or ones but you have yet to give the reader a glimpse of what they are up against. So whether it be a chapter or so later or even a scene later you would use this to display how much more powerful they are as well as the difference in their ideologies as they are pitted against a threat to themselves. Now the reader has a clear picture of what this protagonist is up against or at least to some extent as you don't have to completely let the cat out of the bag. Even though it may not further the plot, it can add value to your story. Another thing is that it allows the reader to compare and contrast the two characters. Aside from this is it can help with foreshadowing.

Example:

In one of R.A. Salvatore's books of his iconic character Drizzit there is a particular scene where he focuses on a dragon. It is not just any dragon but a dragon from the realm of shadow and a very powerful one at that. While the description is not necessarily in depth it clearly leaves you with the idea that this dragon is not something you want to go up against even if you had a considerable size army. However, that is exactly what would have to be done in the end, in order for his long time dwarven friend to reclaim his long-lost home. Aside from that, I don't recall much more being said about the dragon until the big fight at the end but what else needed to be said. The reason I am bringing this up is because it conveys what I have spoken about the authors objective. You clearly realize the dragon is very powerful and dangerous and it is further conveyed during the big fight in the end.

WHY

One reason to implement this is as a subtle tip off from the author to the reader that something wicked this way comes. As mentioned above it works well to juxtapose the situation of one character as opposed to another. And again, just to bring greater attention to something in particular such as a character's nature, especially if it is important to the plot. It all depends on what your intentions are, you may be surprised how often you actually utilize this.

HOW

Something to keep in mind is that this will not be applied to every scene but the scenes you feel that it is necessary.

Example:

Let's say that you have already shown your reader how powerful or weak your protagonist is. Next whether it is a scene or scenes later we introduce the antagonist for the first time. In this scene your aim would be to establish with the reader, a clear contrast between this character and the protagonist. You could focus on things such as the difference in ideologies, desires, goals, strengths, passions and so on. Your reader will now have a greater appreciation for that goal the hero or heroine is out to accomplish or perhaps they may side with the villain and his ideas feeling that they are well justified. Whatever the case, it will largely depend on how well you convey these things. It will also give them an idea on what that hero or heroine is really up against. The biggest thing to consider is that this does not have to be done in just one scene. You can spread out this comparison over several scenes each highlighting different aspects of the villain or hero or heroine. The more important those things are to the plot line the more time you should take to bring them out in different situations as each scene plays out. This will also give your characters some predictability as their true nature will be easily seen.

Just remember that everybody has a reason for the things they do. This provides you with an opportunity to lay out that reason in a way that your antagonist can be viewed from a different perspective rather than just being a villain because they do bad things.

PRACTICAL APPLICATION

These are the types of questions you may wish to consider asking yourself under the author objective heading of your scene outline:

1. Is there any foreshadowing that needs to be done in this scene?
2. If so, how can you utilize the location in order to aide in doing so?
3. If so, how can you utilize the internal resistance in order to aide in doing so?
4. Is there anything of significance that needs to be pointed out to the reader in this scene?

5. If so, what elements will aide you in bringing the most attention to it?

Scene Objective

Definition - goal or purpose the character desires to fulfill.

WHEN

You will be frequently utilizing this element because it is the very core of every scene that you will be writing. The most important thing to keep in mind is that a single objective can easily span more than one scene. Why do I say this? The reason is that no matter how badly you desire to get something done there are many times in life the ambiguous Murphy's Law kicks in and stops, slows, or just throws several wrenches into your works. Murphy's Law makes for very interesting scene writing but your characters still need a particular objective they are trying to fulfill as that obstacle or obstacles drags out the fulfillment of said objective. With the introduction of Murphy we will have some added objectives that need more immediate attention. Does this make sense?

WHY

It is the very heart of each scene in your story. It is what gives your characters purpose and your story value. You could consider this a temporary plot. If you would look at it in such a way it will allow you to give more scrutiny to the events you are orchestrating for that scene or scenes. This also makes it easier to stack your scenes so that you provide a domino effect. An objective in one scene can easily become the obstacle that hinders the objective in the next or vice versa. Just give this some thought and see what wonders begin to bubble up in that creative mind of yours.

HOW

To really put this element into play and provide the most value, you need to do some brainstorming. You don't want to be wily nilly about this. Really give it some thought, although you may say but it is just a scene. Your entire story equates to many scenes. This is also where things discussed in the previous chapters about time, perspective, and location are really going to help you out. All those elements play a large role in helping you to establish exactly what the objectives or objective will be for that scene as well as helping to reveal the potential obstacles to those objectives.

Example:

Think about the whole heist scenario I used in Chapter 2. Let's just say the primary location is going to be a street. Now the secondary location will be a particular portion of that street that lies between some apartment buildings and an intersection. In this secondary location aside from the apartment buildings and traffic lights at the intersection, we also have an alley way. Furthermore, during a particular time we have an armored car that will pass this way without fail but the traffic along that street has been congested due to ongoing construction. So, our criminals are some guys that just happen to be down on their luck and live in that neighborhood and for some apparent reason they get the bright idea to pull off a heist to change things around. Is it starting to become clear to you how these other elements are naturally building the foundation of a scene objective? They provide materials to be used to aid you in coming up with one.

While I will not go further in that example, one objective would be for them to rob the armored car. Even if that is the only objective aside from making a clean get away it is easy to realize all the potential things that can and should go wrong. Every hindrance naturally creates another scene objective. So, the best thing to do is to keep it as simple as possible but allow your writing style to determine what that will look like. Personally, I enjoy making things extremely difficult for my characters. Of course, it makes things difficult for me to figure out how they will get out of the messes I put them in, but it is rewarding as well as an interesting challenge for me and them.

PRACTICAL APPLICATION

These are the types of things you will want to take into consideration under the scene objective heading of your scene outline:

1. Think of at least three ways that Murphy can be used to hinder the goal your characters are trying to achieve.
2. How are they likely to react to them?
3. How can you utilize their response as a hindrance to achieving the original goal?
4. What things in the environment can your characters use to negate the impact of Murphy to get back on course?
5. What indigenous characters can be used to help or hinder the goals of your characters?

CHAPTER 8

BRINGING IT TOGETHER

Below you will find an empty guide to assist you in the outlining and planning of your scene. Realize that the questions below each element are simply there to prime the pump. They are by no means all are even some of the questions that you may come up with yourself to get your scene put together. So, don't try to apply them as a formula but use them to stimulate your own thought process to work better for you. In parenthesis I have given you a brief reminder of the focus of each element to help aide you in answering those questions you are coming up with.

If you find that a particular element does not have a significant part in a certain scene, then, feel free to omit it because you may not use them all for every scene. Although, the more you train your mind to compartmentalize your scene through these elements, it will open more opportunities for your creativity.

Below this blank template, you will find one that I have filled out myself just so you can have an example of it in use.

Example Of A Scene Template

ROUGH SKETCH

(QUICK IDEA)

- Just get some scribbles down and don't worry about the details and get an idea of what things should look like.
- Go somewhere with some paper or your phone and begin to record what you see.

DETAILED SKETCH
(LEAVE NO STONE UNTURNED)

- Take those scribbles and start to shape them up into something more definitive.
- Use power point if you can't draw and just start using shapes as real-life representations of things and put a name on them for the purpose of sorting them into the place they should be.
- If you are an artist, then get to drawing my friend.
- Use a drafting program if necessary.
- Combine your imagination with a photo and just redraw or use power point to omit things that should not be. I mean you will be looking at the photo and recreating the image to your specifications on power point, a sheet of paper and so on.

PRIMARY LOCATION
(GENERAL VIEW)
CURRENT EVENTS:

- What is happening overall at this location?
- What is the outcome on the situation from what has happened or is happening from a previous scene?
- What measures have been set in place to deal with it?
- What measures will be set in place if none are?
- How will these measures impact the primary or secondary characters?

SECONDARY LOCATION
(DETAILED VIEW)

- What does it smell like?

- What is the weather like?
- What type of sounds would you hear?
- What type of lighting is there?
- What color is the sky?
- What type of terrain is there?
- What type of people are there?
- What type of animals are there?
- What type of layout does it have?

CHRONOLOGICAL TIME
(SPECIFIC MOMENTS)

- What time of day is it?
- Are there any significant activities taking place?
- Are there any events going on that will impede the goals of the primary or secondary characters?
- How many people will be in certain areas during a specific time?
- Who will those people be?
- How great will their impact be to what goal that the primary or secondary character needs to accomplish?

PARTICULAR TIME
(SPECIAL EVENTS)

- What are the special events that are going on at the location? (Don't limit your mind to just holidays, think board meetings, briefings, meetings in general and so on.)
- Who will be in attendance at these special events?
- What impact will these events have on the location or in the scene?
- How will these events impede or aide your primary or secondary characters?

PRIMARY CHARACTERS
(CHARACTER POINT OF VIEW)

- Who are they?
- Which character will help create the greatest immersion experience at the start of the scene?
- Which character will help create the greatest immersion experience at the middle of the scene?
- Which character will help create the greatest immersion experience at the end of the scene?
- Would the use of a single character achieve the greatest immersion experience for this scene?

INDIGENOUS CHARACTERS
(BACKGROUND PEOPLE)

- Who are they?
- How many are necessary?
- At what time would certain characters be expected to be at certain places?
- What would they be doing at these locations?
- How would their activities help or hinder the objective of the primary or secondary characters?

GOD'S EYE VIEW
(ZOOMED OUT VIEW)

- At which point of the scene will this be the most useful?
- What is it you are trying to convey to the reader by doing so?

CHARACTER POINT OF VIEW
(FIRST PERSON VIEW)

- Refer to questions under primary character element.

INTERNAL RESISTANCE
(MENTAL TURMOIL)

- What is it?
- What things in the environment could be factors that deepen the impact of the internal resistance?

- How would they be used to do so?
- How does the chronological time play a role in its effect on the internal resistance?
- How does the particular time play a role in its effect on the internal resistance, such as the actual event or events taking place?
- How many indigenous characters will be used to affect the internal resistance?
- How will they be used to do so?

EXTERNAL RESISTANCE
(LOCATION BASED OBSTACLES)

- What is it?
- How many things in this location will be useful in hindering/aiding the primary character?
- In what way will they be used to do so?
- How many indigenous characters will be useful in hindering/helping the primary character?
- What role do they play in that scene or location in general?
- In what way will they be used to do so?
- How many secondary characters will be useful in hindering/helping the primary character?
- What role do they play in that scene or location in general?
- In what way will they be used to do so?

AUTHOR OBJECTIVE
(FORESHADOWING/EMPHASIS)

- What is it?
- Is there any foreshadowing that needs to be done in this scene?
- If so, how can you utilize the location in order to aide in doing so?
- If so, how can you utilize the internal resistance in order to aide in doing so?

- Is there anything of significance that needs to be pointed out to the reader in this scene?

SCENE OBJECTIVE
(CHARACTER GOALS)

- What are the goals of the characters?
- Think of at least three ways that Murphy can be used to hinder the goal your characters are trying to achieve.
- How are they likely to react to them?
- How can you utilize their response to become a hindrance to them achieving their original goal?
- What things in the environment can your characters use to negate the impact of Murphy to get back on course?
- What indigenous characters can be used to help or hinder the goal of your characters?

Example Of A Completed Template

ROUGH SKETCH
(QUICK IDEA)

- Not necessary as I have a printout from on-line that gives me a good layout as to where things are.

DETAILED SKETCH
(LEAVE NO STONE UNTURNED)

- What things from the printout need to be removed?
- I can focus more on this under the secondary location.

PRIMARY LOCATION
(GENERAL VIEW)

- Goulen Industries Moon base

CURRENT SITUATION

- Manitra is sleeping after being knocked out by Dustin but is lying on Felicia's bed in her quarters.
- Paul will either be waiting outside her quarters at some point or just walking into the room as things get explosive between Felicia and Manitra.
- Most likely Paul will be trying to sneak in and catch Felicia still in the shower so he can get an early start on the festivities. Of course, he will never be able to realize what truly awaits him behind that door.
- Felicia will first enter and begin to slightly undress before she enters her bedroom area only to be perplexed by the figure lying on her bed.

SECONDARY LOCATION (DETAILED VIEW)

Felicia's bedroom is where this scene will be taking place. It more precisely will happen within the confined space right around her bed. Manitra will be on the bed sleeping or at least she will appear that way and Felicia will be to the side of the bed checking on her before getting slammed back into the wall.

What kind of lighting is there?

- The lighting will be soft amber-brown type of light.

What does it smell like?

- At first, she will be donned in her chem gear so will not notice the smell of the room until she peels it off and tosses it onto the couch.
- Maybe Felicia notices the smell of both sweat and blood and the redolence of a rose from Manitra's hair in the air. Perhaps it will be gradual as she would be distracted when she first enters but as she lingers it could begin to hit her very strong especially as she moves toward the bedroom area. This could be what leads her to the bedroom.

What does the level of cleanliness look like in the room?

- The room will be very well kept, which is a standard for the base as there are room inspections.

Are there any pictures, trophies, and such?

- Maybe the employees are able to bring a few keepsakes to dress up their rooms, no more than 3 - 6 perhaps. So, she could have a few pictures that are meaningful to her. Maybe there is one of her and Paul at a special place and others of her family or some special keepsake of hers on a dresser or nightstand.

Are there any tables, chairs, dressers and so on and if so, how many?

- There is a couch that can be seen upon the entrance. On the way to the bedroom there is a round table with about three chairs that surround it.
- Perhaps I can add a nightstand next to the bed as well as a small dresser but that would be it. G.I. is very specific on keeping the bare necessities only for the rooms.
- There are no carpets either all rooms are fairly plain in appearance and have the same basic set up. Maybe Felicia could mentally comment on this, that if you have seen one room up here you have seen them all. At least there is no special treatment as far as the rooms are concerned.

What type of floor does it have?

- The floor likely as well as the walls of the entire facility will be made from a nicotine-yellow like plastic.

Does the room have a kitchenette?

- No because eating in the rooms are prohibited. Drinking is the only consumption allowed in the rooms.

Is there any computer or T.V. like devices in the quarters?

- There are no computers permitted because they are only accessible in a specific area in which people are able to take turns

calling down to earth as well as setting up video basedconferences.
- None of the rooms have a t.v. because there is a full theater on site in which a decent amount of movies can be viewed at different times.
- Detailed sketch of Felicia's room:(I used power point for this and modeled it after a picture I downloaded. All of it is custom made. So, don't rule it out as a source for your sketching along with whatever art or drawing programs you may have.)

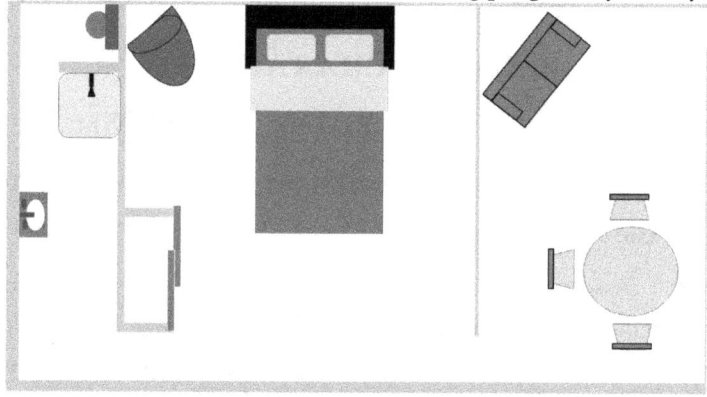

CHRONOLOGICAL TIME
(SPECIFIC MOMENTS)

What time will it be though they are on the moon, morning, afternoon, evening or night?
- On earth it will be around 8:30 a.m. E.S.T.

How many days or hours will have passed since the beat down that she got?
- It will be three days later that she awakens.

Particular time (Special Events)

What are the special events that are going on at the location? (Don't limit your mind to just holidays, think board meetings, briefings, meetings in general and so on.)

- The board meeting will be taking place in a mini conference room.

Who will be in attendance at these special events?

- OP Marshall Johnson will be the only one from the moon base attending the meeting.

What impact will these events have on the location or in the scene?

- The board meeting will not have a direct impact on this scene in particular.

PRIMARY CHARACTERS
(CHARACTER POINT OF VIEW)

Which character will help create the greatest immersion experience at the start of the scene?

- Most of this scene will be from the perspective of Felicia. By doing so it will capture just how feral that Manitra has become now that she feels that she has lost her light. Also, this will help the reader to truly see the fullness of Manitra's broken state and how much that she really does love that little girl.

Which character will help create the greatest immersion experience at the middle of the scene?

- Once again Felicia is the best character and by this point, she will be about to witness Paul's life get snuffed out by Manitra and will likely blurt out something about taking Manitra to see Suzuko. Perhaps she lets the words slip that I will take you to Suzuko which would surely snap Manitra back to her senses and redirect her anger towards her.
- By doing this it will literally save Paul's life. Especially considering that Manitra has not once called her by name so it will be suspicious to her and the reader that this woman knows her name at all.

Which character will help create the greatest immersion experience at the end of the scene?

- Once again Felicia would be the greatest candidate as I could have her briefly hover over Paul, maybe even cradling him for the last time as Manitra growls at her to hurry up. Perhaps she convinces Manitra that she needs to don his suit so that their escape to the shuttle will go smoother considering that the cameras are active.

Would the use of a single character achieve the greatest immersion experience for this scene?

- Yes, just focusing on Felicia will give the best immersion experience.

INDIGENOUS CHARACTERS
(BACKGROUND PEOPLE)

How many are necessary?

- Only Paul and Felicia are necessary.

At what time would certain characters be expected to be at certain places?

- Due to the lock down only guards will be at the assigned infected areas making sure no one is moving around or up to no good.
- Personnel off shift will be gathered in the cafeteria.
- Personnel on shift will be working.

What would they be doing at these locations?

- Does not apply.

How would their activities help or hinder the objective of the primary or secondary characters?

- Does not apply.

GOD'S EYE VIEW
(ZOOMED OUT VIEW)

At which point of the scene will this be the most useful?

- This will likely be used when Felicia first enters her room as I could give a brief overview as to the state that it is in and what it looks like.

What is it you are trying to convey to the reader by doing so?

- Create some general immersion of her room.

INTERNAL RESISTANCE
(MENTAL TURMOIL)

What is the internal resistance the primary or secondary character is facing in this scene?

- Felicia having made it to her room will be at ease about her hygiene since she will be anticipating getting freshened up.
- However, the unexpected meeting with Paul and festivities she has planned goes against her directive. So, the resistance is that she no longer wants to go through with her mission. Also, she realizes how much she still really wants to be with this man although she was angry when he left her behind and put his goals before her. No matter how angry she still feels, her desire for him makes them pale in comparison. So, her state of mind would be that of regret for ever being involved with Pantheon and despising the fate she has been given to be forced to do the one thing she hated him for doing to her.
- So, it needs to be played out through her mind and likely gestures that she is struggling with a very important decision without spilling the beans that she is with Pantheon.

What things in the environment could be factors that deepen the impact of the internal resistance?

- What if there was a very special photo of her and Paul at a memorable location on her table that her line of sight is drawn to.

How would they be used to do so?

- Seeing this picture could bring a mix of emotions roiling up within her. Maybe she stomps over to the table and snatches it up ready to maybe throw it across the room but then just crumples to the floor in tears. It could be at this point perhaps that she notices the peculiar smell in the air now that she would be closer to the next room.

How does the chronological time play a role in its effect on the internal resistance?

- It does not.

How does the particular time play a role in its effect on the internal resistance, such as the actual event or events taking place?

- It does not.

How many indigenous characters will be used to effect the internal resistance?

- One which is Paul.

How will they be used to do so?

- Seeing that Manitra is about to kill Paul gives Felicia the resolve to lose him in order to save him so that will be the event to push her over the edge and follow through with her orders.

How can you use the character perspective to deepen the impact of the internal resistance?

- Getting inside of Felicia's head so the reader can experience her internal struggle as well as temper and mix in talk about her gestures as she does things. That will deepen the feel.

EXTERNAL RESISTANCE
(LOCATION BASED OBSTACLES)

How many things in this location will be useful in hindering/aiding the primary character?

- The things that will assist Manitra will be the walls in the room.

In what way will they be used to do so?

- She will slam Felicia into the nearby wall next to the bed and begin to choke her out before Paul comes rushing in.
- Once he does, she will smash him into the wall behind him and close in to kill him.

How many indigenous characters will be useful in hindering/helping the primary character?

- Paul will be her only real opposition in this scene.

What role do they play in that scene or location in general?

- Manitra is in Felicia's quarters which is why she is there, and Paul is there to have a session with Felicia before his shift ends.

In what way will they be used to do so?

- Felicia is Manitra's ticket off the moon.
- Paul is just a hindrance as well as love interest of Felicia.

How many secondary characters will be useful in hindering/helping the primary character?

- None.

What role do they play in that scene or location in general?

- None.

In what way will they be used to do so?

- None.

AUTHOR OBJECTIVE
(FORESHADOWING/EMPHASIS)

Is there any foreshadowing that needs to be done in this scene?

- None that I can think of.

Is there anything of significance that needs to be pointed out to the reader in this scene?

- The fact that Felicia is with Pantheon, but I don't want to make it very obvious so just enough to help draw the conclusion.

If so, what elements will aide you in bringing the most attention to it?

- Felicia's internal resistance as well as her blurting out that she can take Manitra to Suzuko should be enough to do so without ruining things.

SCENE OBJECTIVE
(CHARACTER GOALS)

Think of at least three ways that Murphy can be used to hinder the goal your characters are trying to achieve.

- In Manitra's mind it is the same day that she got beat down just later. I need to figure out a way to bring that out.
- Felicia will not have been expecting Manitra to be in her room.
- Paul will not have been expecting Felicia to be in trouble.

How are they likely to react to them?

- Manitra will be in a feral state due to loosing Suzuko and only sees red.
- Felicia will be trying to process why Manitra is there and trying to calm her down before she gets fully choked out.
- Paul will just come in guns blazing to protect his Mocha.

How can you utilize their response to hinder them from achieving their original goal?

- Manitra trying to kill Felicia will be a strong hindrance in getting her off the base as well as the involvement of Paul.

- Felicia is trying to carry out her mission although she is debating going through with it and Manitra is still trying to get to Suzuko thinking that she is still there on the base. Due to her feral state she is not using her Zhan Lyn which is very difficult to use in an unbalanced emotional state.

What things in the environment can your characters use to negate the impact of Murphy to get back on course?

- Felicia will need to do something to get Manitra to stop trying to kill Paul so that she can get her off the base as planned.

What indigenous characters can be used to help or hinder the goal of your characters?

- It has already been discussed.

ABOUT THE AUTHOR

J. A. COX enjoys investing into and empowering others with the things that he is knowledgeable in. It brings him great joy to take out the time to help another person understand something that he has an interest in and has put the time into studying and researching, to aide them in gaining a greater perspective on the subject. In the end it is the love of empowering that teaching brings along with it that brings him the greatest joy.